©DISNEY

# A Children's Book About
# STEALING

Managing Editor: Ellen Klarberg
Copy Editor: Annette Gooch
Editorial Assistant: Lana Eberhard
Art Director: Jennifer Wiezel
Production Artist: Gail Miller
Illustration Designer: Bartholomew
Inking Artist: Berenice Happé Iriks
Coloring Artist: Christine McNamara
Lettering Artist: Linda Hanney
Typographer: Communication Graphics

Printed in 1991

A Children's Book About

# STEALING

By Joy Berry

GROLIER ENTERPRISES CORP.

This book is about Karen and her friend Lennie.

Reading about Karen and Lennie can help you understand and deal with **stealing.**

Has anyone ever taken something that belonged to you and not returned it?

You are stealing when you take and keep something that does not belong to you.

If someone steals from you:
- You might feel disappointed, frustrated, and angry.
- You might think that the person cannot be trusted.
- You might not want that person to be near your things.

It is important to treat other people the way you want to be treated.

If you do not want other people to steal from you, you must not steal from them.

Sometimes you might take something *by accident.*

You might borrow something and forget to return it.

You might take something without thinking about it.

The things you take accidentally need to be returned right away.

Sometimes people take things *on purpose.*
They know what they are doing. They
choose to steal.

Sometimes people steal *because they want something or because they think they need something.* They might think that they cannot be happy unless they have the thing they are stealing.

Sometimes people steal *because their friends steal.*

They might think it is OK to steal because their friends do it.

They might not want to be different from their friends who steal.

They might think their friends will like them better if they steal.

Sometimes people steal *because they think what they do will not make a difference.* They think no one will notice. They tell themselves their stealing will not hurt anyone.

Sometimes people steal *because they are angry.* They want to get back at someone who has done something to hurt them.

Stealing is wrong. No matter why people do it, it is never OK to take something that does not belong to you.

Try to make things right if you have stolen anything. Return what you have stolen if it is not broken or ruined.

If it is broken or ruined, replace it or pay for it.

Tell the person you stole from that you are sorry. Then do not steal again.

It is important to treat other people the way you want to be treated.

If you do not want other people to steal from you, you must not steal from them.